Driving Disruption Startups Paving the Way for Future Transportation

Saba

1

TABLE OF CONTENTS

Chapter 1: Introduction to the Future of Transportation

The Importance of Transportation in Society

Transportation plays a vital role in society, and its significance cannot be overlooked. It is the backbone that connects people, goods, and ideas, facilitating economic growth and societal development. In the fast-paced world we live in, transportation has become a necessity, and its future is brimming with transformative potential.

As startups in the transportation industry, you are at the forefront of shaping the future of transportation. The challenges we face today, such as traffic congestion, environmental concerns, and the need for efficient and sustainable mobility solutions, call for innovative approaches and disruptive ideas. Your startups hold the key to unlocking a future where transportation is smarter, greener, and more accessible than ever before.

One of the crucial aspects of transportation is its ability to connect people and foster social interactions. Whether it's commuting to work, traveling to meet loved ones, or exploring new places, transportation brings people together. Startups have the opportunity to revolutionize the way people move, making travel more convenient, comfortable, and personalized. By leveraging technology and data, you can create seamless and on-demand transportation experiences that cater to individual preferences and needs.

Additionally, transportation is a vital component of economic growth. Efficient movement of goods and services is essential for businesses to thrive. Startups in the transportation sector can streamline logistics and supply chains, reducing costs and improving productivity. By leveraging automation, artificial intelligence, and innovative delivery models, you can create a more efficient and sustainable ecosystem that benefits businesses and consumers alike.

Furthermore, transportation has a significant impact on the environment. As the world grapples with climate change and its consequences, finding sustainable transportation solutions has become imperative. Startups have the unique opportunity to develop eco-friendly alternatives to traditional modes of transportation, such as electric vehicles, shared mobility platforms, and intelligent transportation systems. By prioritizing sustainability, you can contribute to a greener future and mitigate the environmental impact of transportation.

In conclusion, transportation is a fundamental pillar of society, and its importance cannot be overstated. As startups in the transportation industry, you have the power to revolutionize the way we move and shape the future of transportation. By addressing challenges, embracing innovation, and prioritizing sustainability, you can pave the way for a future where transportation is more efficient, accessible, and environmentally friendly. Your work has the potential to transform the lives of individuals, businesses, and communities worldwide. Embrace this opportunity and drive the disruption necessary to create a brighter future for transportation.

Trends and Challenges in the Transportation Industry

As the world continues to evolve, so does the transportation industry. In recent years, we have witnessed significant advancements that are reshaping the way we move from one place to another. This subchapter aims to highlight some of the most prominent trends and challenges that startups in the transportation industry need to be aware of in order to thrive in the future.

One of the most notable trends in the transportation industry is the rise of electric vehicles (EVs). With growing concerns about climate change and environmental sustainability, governments and consumers are increasingly favoring EVs over traditional gasoline-powered cars. Startups in the transportation industry need to recognize this trend and capitalize on it by developing innovative EV technology, creating charging infrastructure, and offering EV-related services.

Another trend that has gained momentum is the concept of shared mobility. Traditional car ownership is becoming less popular, especially among younger generations who prioritize convenience and cost-effectiveness. Startups in the transportation industry can tap into this trend by offering shared mobility solutions such as ride-hailing, car-sharing, and bike-sharing services. By embracing this trend, startups have the opportunity to disrupt the traditional transportation model and provide more sustainable and efficient options for consumers.

However, along with these trends come a set of challenges that startups must navigate. One of the biggest challenges is the need for regulation and policy changes. As new transportation technologies emerge, governments and regulatory bodies are struggling to keep up with the pace of innovation. Startups need to actively engage with policymakers to advocate for regulations that foster innovation while ensuring safety and fair competition.

Another challenge is the integration of emerging technologies such as autonomous vehicles (AVs) and drones into the transportation ecosystem. While AVs and drones have the potential to revolutionize the industry, their widespread adoption requires significant investment in infrastructure, public acceptance, and addressing ethical concerns. Startups need to address these challenges by collaborating with stakeholders, conducting rigorous testing, and building public trust.

In conclusion, the transportation industry is witnessing transformative trends that present both opportunities and challenges for startups. By recognizing and embracing trends such as electric vehicles and shared mobility, startups can position themselves at the forefront of innovation. However, they must also navigate challenges related to regulation, policy changes, and the integration of emerging technologies. By overcoming these obstacles, startups have the potential to drive disruption and pave the way for the future of transportation.

The Role of Startups in Driving Disruption

In today's ever-evolving world, startups play a crucial role in driving disruption, particularly in the realm of transportation. The traditional transportation industry is undergoing a significant transformation, and it is the startups that are paving the way for the future. This subchapter explores the vital role that startups play in driving disruption in the transportation sector and why they are at the forefront of innovation.

Startups are known for their agility and ability to think outside the box. They bring a fresh perspective to the table, unencumbered by the constraints of legacy systems and established norms. This allows them to identify gaps in the market and develop innovative solutions that address unmet needs. Startups have the freedom to experiment, fail fast, and iterate quickly, which is essential in an industry that demands constant adaptation to changing consumer preferences and technological advancements.

One of the key areas where startups are making a significant impact is in the development of sustainable transportation solutions. With the growing concerns over climate change and the need to reduce carbon emissions, startups are leading the charge in providing greener alternatives. From electric vehicles to shared mobility platforms, startups are developing innovative ways to reduce the environmental footprint of transportation while still meeting the mobility needs of consumers.

Startups are also disrupting the traditional concept of transportation through the development of autonomous vehicles and advanced mobility technologies. They are leveraging artificial intelligence, machine learning, and big data analytics to create intelligent transportation systems that are safer, more efficient, and more convenient. By embracing these technologies, startups are redefining the future of transportation and revolutionizing the way people move from one place to another.

Moreover, startups are driving disruption by challenging the dominance of established players in the industry. They are disrupting existing business models and reimagining the entire transportation ecosystem. Through their disruptive innovations, startups are forcing incumbents to adapt, evolve, and innovate to stay relevant in an ever-changing landscape.

To thrive in this disruptive environment, startups need to embrace a culture of collaboration, experimentation, and constant learning. They need to be open to partnerships with other startups, established companies, and government entities to leverage resources, expertise, and scale. By working together, startups can accelerate the pace of disruption and create a future of transportation that is more sustainable, efficient, and accessible for everyone.

Conclusion,

startups have a pivotal role to play in driving disruption in the transportation industry. Their agility, innovative mindset, and willingness to challenge the status quo make them indispensable in shaping the future of transportation. By embracing sustainability, advanced technologies, and collaboration, startups can lead the way in transforming the way we travel and revolutionize the transportation sector as a whole.

Chapter 2: The Rise of Electric Vehicles

Advancements in Battery Technology

The future of transportation is undergoing a massive transformation, and startups are at the forefront of driving this disruption. As the world moves towards a more sustainable and efficient transportation system, one of the key areas of focus is battery technology. This subchapter delves into the latest advancements in battery technology and how startups are paving the way for a new era of transportation.

Battery technology plays a pivotal role in the development of electric vehicles (EVs) and other sustainable modes of transportation. Over the years, there have been significant advancements in battery technology that have revolutionized the industry. Startups have been instrumental in pushing the boundaries and accelerating the adoption of these innovations.

One noteworthy advancement is the development of high-energy density batteries. Startups have been working tirelessly to improve the energy storage capacity of batteries, allowing for longer range and extended battery life in electric vehicles. These advancements have addressed one of the major concerns for EV adoption and have made them a viable alternative to traditional combustion engines.

Furthermore, startups are focused on developing fast-charging technologies. The ability to charge an electric vehicle quickly is crucial for the widespread adoption of EVs. Startups are leveraging cutting-edge technologies such as solid-state batteries and advanced charging infrastructure to reduce charging times significantly. This breakthrough is enabling the integration of EVs into our daily lives seamlessly.

Another area of advancement in battery technology is the development of sustainable and eco-friendly batteries. Startups are exploring alternative materials and manufacturing processes that reduce the environmental impact of batteries. From using recycled materials to developing biodegradable batteries, these startups are ensuring that the future of transportation is not only efficient but also sustainable.

Moreover, startups are actively working on improving the safety and reliability of batteries. By implementing advanced safety features and developing robust battery management systems, startups are addressing the concerns regarding battery fires and overall reliability. These advancements are crucial in building trust among consumers and accelerating the transition to electric vehicles.

In conclusion, the advancements in battery technology are propelling the future of transportation towards a more sustainable and efficient system. Startups are playing a pivotal role in pushing the boundaries and revolutionizing battery technology. From high-energy density batteries to fast-charging technologies and sustainable alternatives, these startups are driving the disruption in the transportation industry. As the world embraces a greener future, it is these startups that will pave the way and shape the future of transportation.

Electric Vehicle Infrastructure

As the world moves towards a more sustainable future, electric vehicles (EVs) have become a vital part of the transportation ecosystem. With their zero-emission capabilities and potential for reducing carbon footprints, EVs are poised to revolutionize the way we commute and travel. However, for this transformation to truly take place, a robust electric vehicle infrastructure is crucial.

The development of an extensive charging network is at the forefront of building this infrastructure. Startups in the future of transportation niche have a unique opportunity to contribute to the growth of this network. By investing in the creation of charging stations and innovative charging solutions, startups can help overcome one of the major hurdles for mass EV adoption – range anxiety. Collaborating with governments, businesses, and communities, these startups can create a seamless charging experience, encouraging more individuals and businesses to switch to electric vehicles.

Furthermore, startups can also focus on developing smart grid technologies that can efficiently manage the energy demand of EV charging. By integrating renewable energy sources and energy storage systems, startups can ensure that EV charging does not strain the existing power infrastructure. This would not only promote sustainability but also contribute to building a more resilient and reliable energy grid.

Another area where startups can make a significant impact is in the development of advanced battery technologies. Improving the range, charging speed, and longevity of EV batteries can accelerate the adoption of electric vehicles. Startups can explore innovative materials, manufacturing processes, and recycling techniques to make batteries more efficient, cost-effective, and environmentally friendly.

In addition to charging infrastructure and battery technologies, startups can also focus on developing software platforms and applications that enhance the overall EV experience. From mobile apps that locate charging stations to platforms that enable seamless payment and data integration, startups have the potential to simplify the EV ownership process and make it more convenient for consumers.

As the demand for electric vehicles grows, it is essential for startups to collaborate and create partnerships to accelerate the development of the electric vehicle infrastructure. By leveraging their expertise, agility, and innovation, startups can play a pivotal role in shaping the future of transportation and driving the disruption towards a sustainable and electrified world.

Startups Revolutionizing the Electric Vehicle Market

The electric vehicle (EV) industry is experiencing a monumental shift, and startups are at the forefront of this revolution. Their innovative ideas, disruptive technologies, and unique business models are paving the way for a future where sustainable transportation is the norm. In this subchapter, we will explore some of the most exciting startups that are driving this disruption and shaping the future of transportation.

1. Tesla: No discussion about EV startups can begin without mentioning Tesla. This iconic company has not only made electric vehicles cool but has also redefined the entire automotive industry. With their cutting-edge technology, long-range batteries, and sleek designs, Tesla has set new benchmarks for performance and range in the EV market.

2. Rivian: Rivian is an American startup that aims to revolutionize the electric pickup truck and SUV segment. Their vehicles combine ruggedness, utility, and sustainability, appealing to adventure enthusiasts and environmentally conscious consumers alike. Rivian has garnered significant attention and investments, making it one of the most promising startups in the EV space.

3. NIO: NIO is a Chinese startup that is making waves in the electric vehicle market. With a focus on premium electric SUVs, NIO offers advanced features like swappable batteries, autonomous driving capabilities, and a seamless charging infrastructure. Their emphasis on user experience has earned

them a loyal customer base and positions them as a major player in the future of transportation.

4. BYD: Backed by Warren Buffett, BYD is a Chinese startup that has quickly become one of the world's largest EV manufacturers. They specialize in electric buses, which are becoming increasingly popular in urban transportation. BYD's innovative battery technology and commitment to sustainability have made them a leader in the global EV market.

5. Bird: While not an electric vehicle manufacturer, Bird is disrupting the transportation industry with its electric scooters. This startup allows users to rent and ride electric scooters through a smartphone app, providing a convenient and eco-friendly alternative for short-distance travel in urban areas. Bird's success has inspired numerous other scooter-sharing startups and highlights the potential for micro-mobility solutions in the future.

These startups are just a glimpse of the incredible innovation happening in the electric vehicle market. Their disruptive ideas are reshaping the way we think about transportation and accelerating the adoption of sustainable alternatives. As a startup in the transportation industry, it is crucial to take inspiration from these visionaries and find ways to contribute to this revolution. By embracing technology, sustainability, and user-centric design, startups can play a vital role in shaping the future of transportation and driving the next wave of disruption in the EV market.

Chapter 3: Autonomous Vehicles: Shaping the Future of Transportation

Understanding Autonomous Vehicle Technology

In recent years, autonomous vehicles have emerged as a revolutionary technology that is set to disrupt the transportation industry like never before. This subchapter aims to provide startups in the transportation industry with an in-depth understanding of autonomous vehicle technology and its implications for the future of transportation.

Autonomous vehicle technology refers to the ability of a vehicle to operate without human intervention. It is powered by a combination of advanced sensors, artificial intelligence, and sophisticated algorithms that enable the vehicle to perceive its environment, make decisions, and navigate safely.

One of the key components of autonomous vehicle technology is the sensors. These sensors, such as cameras, radar, lidar, and ultrasonic sensors, continuously scan the vehicle's surroundings, capturing data about other vehicles, pedestrians, and road conditions. This data is then processed by the vehicle's AI system, which makes real-time decisions based on the information received.

The AI system in autonomous vehicles utilizes deep learning algorithms to analyze the data collected by the sensors and make decisions accordingly. These algorithms enable the vehicle to recognize and interpret objects, predict their behavior, and plan the appropriate response. The more data an autonomous vehicle collects and analyzes, the smarter and more efficient it becomes.

The implications of autonomous vehicle technology for the future of transportation are vast. With autonomous vehicles, the concept of car ownership is set to change. Instead of owning a personal vehicle, individuals will have access to on-demand autonomous vehicles, providing a more cost-effective and convenient alternative to traditional car ownership.

Moreover, autonomous vehicles have the potential to greatly enhance road safety. The AI systems in these vehicles are designed to minimize human errors and react much faster than humans in potentially dangerous situations. This could lead to a significant reduction in accidents and fatalities on the roads.

In addition to safety benefits, autonomous vehicles also offer environmental advantages. The AI systems can optimize routes, reduce traffic congestion, and minimize fuel consumption, leading to a decrease in greenhouse gas emissions and a more sustainable transportation system.

As startups in the transportation industry, it is crucial to understand the intricacies of autonomous vehicle technology. By embracing this disruptive technology, startups can create innovative solutions that leverage autonomous vehicles to transform the way people and goods move from one place to another.

In the following chapters, we will explore the various startups that are already paving the way for the future of transportation by harnessing the power of autonomous vehicle technology. This will provide valuable insights and inspiration for startups looking to enter this exciting and rapidly evolving field.

The Impact of Autonomous Vehicles on Society

In recent years, the emergence of autonomous vehicles has revolutionized the transportation industry. This chapter explores the profound impact these vehicles have on society, particularly in terms of safety, accessibility, and environmental sustainability. As startups in the field of future transportation, understanding these implications can help you navigate the exciting opportunities and challenges that lie ahead.

One of the most significant benefits of autonomous vehicles is the potential to significantly enhance road safety. With advanced sensors and artificial intelligence, these vehicles have the ability to avoid human errors, which are responsible for the majority of accidents on our roads. By eliminating human factors like fatigue, distraction, and impaired driving, autonomous vehicles have the potential to save countless lives and reduce injuries. This not only improves the overall safety of transportation but also presents a promising opportunity for startups to develop innovative safety technologies and systems.

Furthermore, the advent of autonomous vehicles promises to revolutionize accessibility for various segments of society. Elderly individuals, people with disabilities, and those without access to traditional transportation options can greatly benefit from the increased mobility provided by autonomous vehicles. Startups can explore the development of specialized vehicles or services tailored to the unique needs of these individuals, fostering a more inclusive and equitable transportation system.

Another crucial aspect of autonomous vehicles is their potential to address environmental concerns. Electric-powered autonomous vehicles have the ability to reduce greenhouse gas emissions, contributing to a more sustainable future. With the rise of electric vehicle infrastructure, startups can seize the opportunity to develop charging solutions, battery technologies, or even renewable energy integration strategies to support the widespread adoption of autonomous electric vehicles. This not only aligns with the growing trend towards environmental consciousness but also opens up new avenues for startups to disrupt the transportation industry.

While the impact of autonomous vehicles on society is promising, it is not without its challenges. Ethical dilemmas, regulatory frameworks, and public acceptance are just a few of the hurdles that need to be overcome. As startups in the field of future transportation, it is vital to stay informed, collaborate with policymakers, and actively engage with communities to ensure that the deployment of autonomous vehicles is done in a responsible and ethical manner.

In conclusion, the impact of autonomous vehicles on society is transformative. By improving safety, accessibility, and sustainability, these vehicles hold the potential to revolutionize transportation as we know it. As startups paving the way for future transportation, understanding these implications allows you to seize the endless opportunities and contribute to a better future for all.

Startups Leading the Way in Autonomous Vehicle Development

In recent years, the world has witnessed a rapid advancement in autonomous vehicle technology. As traditional automakers and tech giants compete to dominate this emerging market, it is the startups that are truly leading the way in driving disruption in the future of transportation. These innovative companies are not only reshaping the automotive industry but also revolutionizing the way we commute, travel, and interact with vehicles.

One such startup that has made significant strides in autonomous vehicle development is Waymo. Formerly known as the Google Self-Driving Car Project, Waymo has been at the forefront of the industry since its inception in 2009. With a deep focus on building the most advanced self-driving technology, Waymo has successfully logged millions of autonomous miles on public roads. Their dedication to safety and extensive testing has earned them a reputation as one of the leaders in the autonomous vehicle space.

Another startup that deserves recognition is Zoox. Established in 2014, Zoox aims to create a fleet of fully autonomous, electric vehicles for ride-sharing purposes. What sets Zoox apart is their emphasis on designing purpose-built vehicles from scratch, without the constraints of retrofitting existing cars. By taking a holistic approach to autonomous vehicle development, Zoox is well-positioned to disrupt the transportation industry and redefine the future of mobility.

Cruise, a San Francisco-based startup acquired by General Motors, is another key player in this space. Focused on building self-driving cars that can be used for ride-sharing, Cruise has made significant progress in developing a scalable autonomous vehicle platform. With a mission to provide safer, cleaner, and more accessible transportation, Cruise has attracted substantial investment and partnerships, further solidifying their position as a leading force in autonomous vehicle development.

Startups like Nuro are also making a significant impact on the future of transportation. Founded by two former Google engineers, Nuro is revolutionizing the last-mile delivery industry by developing fully autonomous delivery vehicles. By removing the need for human drivers, Nuro's vehicles can efficiently navigate urban environments, reducing congestion and emissions while increasing the efficiency of deliveries.

These are just a few examples of the startups that are paving the way for future transportation. Their relentless pursuit of innovation, combined with their agility and ability to challenge the status quo, has enabled them to disrupt the automotive industry and redefine the way we think about transportation. As startups in the transportation niche, it is crucial to stay informed about these trailblazing companies and learn from their successes and failures. By embracing the spirit of disruption and continuously pushing the boundaries of autonomous vehicle development, startups can position themselves as key players in shaping the future of transportation.

Chapter 4: Mobility as a Service (MaaS)

The Concept of Mobility as a Service

In recent years, the transportation industry has witnessed a paradigm shift with the rise of Mobility as a Service (MaaS). As startups continue to pave the way for the future of transportation, understanding the concept of MaaS becomes crucial. This subchapter delves into the core principles and potential of MaaS, offering startups in the transportation niche a comprehensive overview.

At its essence, MaaS is a revolutionary approach that seeks to integrate various modes of transportation into a single, seamless service. By combining public transport, ride-hailing, bike-sharing, car-sharing, and other mobility options, MaaS aims to provide users with a convenient and efficient way to navigate urban environments. Gone are the days of relying on multiple apps and services; MaaS envisions a future where users can plan, book, and pay for their entire journey with a single platform.

The benefits of MaaS are numerous. For startups in the transportation sector, embracing this concept opens up a world of opportunities. By offering an integrated MaaS solution, startups can attract customers who are seeking a more convenient, cost-effective, and sustainable way to travel. Moreover, MaaS has the potential to significantly reduce congestion, lower carbon emissions, and improve overall transport efficiency in urban areas.

To successfully implement MaaS, startups must overcome various challenges. These include technical integration, data sharing, regulatory hurdles, and collaboration among different stakeholders in the transportation ecosystem. However, the rewards far outweigh the obstacles. By embracing MaaS, startups can position themselves at the forefront of the future of transportation, disrupting traditional models and reshaping urban mobility.

Startups in the transportation sector should consider partnering with other players in the industry, including public transport authorities, vehicle manufacturers, technology providers, and local governments. Collaborative efforts can help create a robust MaaS ecosystem that benefits all stakeholders involved.

In conclusion, the concept of Mobility as a Service holds immense potential for startups in the transportation sector. By offering a seamless, integrated solution that encompasses various modes of transport, startups can revolutionize urban mobility. Overcoming challenges through collaboration and innovation will be key to driving the adoption of MaaS and paving the way for the future of transportation. Embrace MaaS today, and position your startup at the forefront of driving disruption in the transportation industry.

Benefits and Challenges of MaaS

In recent years, the concept of Mobility as a Service (MaaS) has gained significant attention in the field of transportation. MaaS refers to the integration of various transportation services into a single platform, offering users a seamless and convenient travel experience. This subchapter will delve into the benefits and challenges associated with MaaS, addressing startups operating in the future of transportation niche.

Benefits of MaaS:

1. Enhanced Convenience: One of the primary advantages of MaaS is the convenience it offers to users. With a single platform, individuals can easily plan, book, and pay for multiple transportation modes, such as buses, trains, taxis, and bike-sharing services. This integrated approach eliminates the need for juggling multiple apps and provides a seamless travel experience.

2. Cost Savings: MaaS can potentially provide cost savings for both users and transportation providers. By offering various transportation options, MaaS enables users to choose the most cost-effective mode of travel. Additionally, it allows transportation providers to optimize their operations by efficiently allocating resources and reducing empty vehicle miles.

3. Reduced Congestion and Emissions: MaaS has the potential to reduce traffic congestion and greenhouse gas emissions by promoting the use of shared modes of transportation. By encouraging users to choose public transportation, carpooling, or

shared mobility services, MaaS can contribute to a more sustainable and efficient transportation system.

4. Improved Accessibility: MaaS can greatly improve accessibility for individuals with limited mobility or those living in underserved areas. By integrating various transportation options, MaaS ensures that individuals have access to a wide range of services, regardless of their location or physical abilities.

Challenges of MaaS:

1. Technological Integration: Implementing MaaS requires extensive technological integration between various transportation services and systems. Startups operating in this space need to overcome interoperability challenges, ensuring that different platforms can seamlessly communicate with each other.

2. Regulatory Framework: The success of MaaS depends on a supportive regulatory framework that facilitates collaboration between different stakeholders. Startups in the future of transportation niche need to navigate the complexities of regulations, ensuring compliance while advocating for policies that foster innovation and competition.

3. Privacy and Security Concerns: MaaS involves the collection and processing of vast amounts of personal data. Startups must address privacy and security concerns to build trust with users and ensure the protection of their sensitive information.

4. Changing User Behavior: Encouraging users to adopt MaaS and shift from private vehicles to shared modes of transportation can be challenging. Startups need to design user-friendly interfaces, provide incentives, and effectively communicate the benefits of MaaS to change user behavior and promote its adoption.

In conclusion, MaaS holds immense potential to revolutionize the future of transportation. Startups operating in this niche have the opportunity to capitalize on the benefits of MaaS, such as enhanced convenience, cost savings, reduced congestion, and improved accessibility. However, they must also navigate challenges related to technological integration, regulatory frameworks, privacy and security concerns, and changing user behavior. By addressing these challenges and leveraging the benefits, startups can drive the disruption in the transportation industry and pave the way for a more sustainable and efficient future.

Startups Transforming the Mobility as a Service Industry

In recent years, the transportation industry has witnessed a significant shift towards a more sustainable and efficient future. This transformation has been largely driven by startups that are redefining how people move from one place to another. These disruptors are collectively known as the Mobility as a Service (MaaS) startups, and they are revolutionizing the way we think about transportation.

MaaS startups are leveraging technology, data, and innovative business models to provide seamless, convenient, and sustainable transportation options to individuals and communities. They are challenging the traditional modes of transportation, such as private car ownership, and are offering viable alternatives that are cost-effective and environmentally friendly.

One of the key players in this space is ride-sharing platforms like Uber and Lyft. These startups have disrupted the taxi industry by providing on-demand and affordable transportation services through their mobile applications. By utilizing underutilized private vehicles, they have reduced congestion and emissions, making urban mobility more efficient.

Another notable startup is Lime, which offers electric scooters and bikes for short-distance travel. Lime's dockless system allows users to easily locate and rent their electric vehicles through a smartphone app. This innovative solution has gained popularity in urban areas, as it provides a convenient and sustainable option for short trips, reducing the reliance on cars.

Shared mobility startups like Zipcar and Car2Go are also making waves in the MaaS industry. These companies provide car-sharing services, allowing individuals to rent vehicles for a short period. By offering an alternative to car ownership, these startups are promoting a more sustainable and efficient use of vehicles, reducing the number of cars on the road and decreasing congestion.

Furthermore, startups like Bird and Skip are transforming the last-mile transportation segment. They offer electric scooters that can be easily rented and used for short journeys, bridging the gap between public transportation stops and final destinations. These innovative solutions are not only convenient but also contribute to reducing traffic congestion and improving air quality.

Overall, MaaS startups are reshaping the future of transportation by providing innovative and sustainable solutions. Their disruptive technologies and business models are challenging the status quo and paving the way for a more efficient, convenient, and environmentally friendly transportation system. As startups in the transportation industry, it is crucial to keep an eye on these transformative companies as they are shaping the future of mobility and setting new standards for the industry. Embracing their innovative ideas and leveraging emerging technologies can help startups thrive and contribute to the future of transportation.

Chapter 5: Sustainable Transportation Solutions

The Need for Sustainable Transportation

In today's rapidly evolving world, the future of transportation is a crucial topic that demands our attention. As startups in the transportation industry, it is essential for us to understand the urgent need for sustainable transportation solutions. This subchapter delves into the reasons why sustainable transportation is not only desirable but also imperative for the future of our planet and the success of our startups.

First and foremost, the environmental impact of traditional transportation is undeniable. The burning of fossil fuels and the emissions generated by conventional vehicles contribute significantly to climate change. As startups working towards the future of transportation, we have a responsibility to minimize our carbon footprint and develop innovative solutions that reduce greenhouse gas emissions. By embracing sustainable transportation, we can play a pivotal role in combating climate change and preserving our planet for future generations.

Moreover, sustainable transportation presents a unique opportunity for startups to differentiate themselves in a crowded market. With consumers becoming increasingly conscious of their environmental impact, there is a growing demand for eco-friendly transportation options. By offering sustainable alternatives such as electric vehicles, car-sharing platforms, or efficient public transportation systems, startups can attract a new wave of environmentally conscious customers. Embracing sustainability not only benefits the planet but also opens up significant business opportunities for startups willing to adapt.

Furthermore, sustainable transportation can lead to economic growth and job creation. As the demand for sustainable transportation solutions rises, so does the need for skilled professionals to develop and maintain these systems. By investing in sustainable transportation initiatives, startups can contribute to economic development in their communities and create new employment opportunities. This not only strengthens the startup ecosystem but also fosters positive social change.

Lastly, sustainable transportation is a key element in building smart cities of the future. By integrating technology, renewable energy sources, and efficient transportation systems, startups can play a pivotal role in creating livable and sustainable urban environments. Smart transportation solutions, such as intelligent traffic management systems, can reduce congestion, enhance safety, and improve overall quality of life for city dwellers. By being at the forefront of sustainable transportation innovation, startups can shape the cities of tomorrow.

In conclusion, the need for sustainable transportation is undeniable. As startups in the transportation industry, we have a unique opportunity to lead the way towards a greener future. By embracing sustainability, we can address pressing environmental concerns, seize business opportunities, contribute to economic growth, and shape the cities of the future. Let us embark on this journey together, driving disruption and paving the way for a sustainable and prosperous future of transportation.

Startups Innovating in Sustainable Transportation

Subchapter: Startups Innovating in Sustainable Transportation

Introduction:

In recent years, the future of transportation has witnessed a remarkable shift towards sustainability. Startups have played a pivotal role in driving this disruption by introducing innovative solutions that address the environmental challenges associated with conventional modes of transportation. This subchapter explores the groundbreaking efforts of startups to create a more sustainable transportation landscape and highlights the opportunities available for aspiring entrepreneurs in this niche.

1. Electrification:
One of the most notable trends in sustainable transportation is the electrification of vehicles. Startups have been at the forefront of developing electric cars, bikes, scooters, and even trucks. They are leveraging advancements in battery technology, charging infrastructure, and software to make electric vehicles more accessible, affordable, and efficient. These startups are revolutionizing the way we think about transportation and reducing our dependence on fossil fuels.

2. Shared Mobility:
Another area where startups are driving sustainable transportation is through shared mobility services. Companies like Uber and Lyft have transformed the way we move by utilizing the concept of the sharing economy. Startups are taking this idea further by offering shared electric scooters, bikes, and even cars.

By promoting the use of shared vehicles, these startups are reducing congestion, lowering emissions, and making transportation more affordable for everyone.

3. Alternative Fuels: Startups are also exploring alternative fuels beyond electricity. From biofuels to hydrogen, these entrepreneurs are developing innovative solutions that reduce carbon emissions and promote a sustainable transportation ecosystem. By leveraging advanced research and development, startups are making alternative fuels more viable and cost-effective, thus challenging the dominance of fossil fuels.

4. Autonomous Transportation: Autonomous vehicles are poised to revolutionize transportation in the future. Startups are actively working on self-driving cars and trucks that promise safer, more efficient, and environmentally friendly transportation. By eliminating human error, autonomous vehicles can optimize routes, reduce congestion, and ultimately lower emissions. Startups in this niche are pushing the boundaries of technology and paving the way for a more sustainable future.

Conclusion:
The future of transportation lies in sustainability, and startups are driving this disruption. By innovating in areas like electrification, shared mobility, alternative fuels, and autonomous transportation, these startups are transforming the way we commute, reducing our carbon footprint, and shaping a more

sustainable future for transportation. Aspiring entrepreneurs in the field of sustainable transportation have a unique opportunity to make a significant impact by developing innovative solutions that address the challenges of the present and pave the way for a greener future.

Government Policies and Regulations Supporting Sustainable Transportation Startups

In recent years, there has been a significant shift towards sustainable transportation solutions as the world grapples with the challenges of climate change and the need to reduce carbon emissions. This shift has created a fertile ground for startups aiming to disrupt the transportation industry by offering innovative, environmentally friendly alternatives. However, navigating the complex web of government policies and regulations can be a daunting task for these startups. Fortunately, governments around the world are recognizing the importance of sustainable transportation and are implementing policies and regulations to support and encourage these startups.

One of the most significant ways governments are supporting sustainable transportation startups is through financial incentives. Many countries and local governments provide grants, subsidies, and tax breaks to startups that are working on sustainable transportation solutions. These financial incentives help startups overcome the initial hurdles of research and development, manufacturing, and marketing, allowing them to bring their products and services to market more quickly and effectively.

Additionally, governments are implementing policies that prioritize sustainable transportation solutions in public procurement. This means that startups offering sustainable transportation alternatives have a better chance of securing contracts with government agencies and municipalities. This not only provides startups with a steady revenue stream but also acts as a seal of approval, boosting their credibility and attracting more customers.

Furthermore, governments are introducing regulations that promote the adoption of sustainable transportation solutions. For instance, stricter emissions standards are being implemented, which put traditional transportation companies under pressure to reduce their carbon footprint or face penalties. This creates a level playing field for startups that have already embraced sustainability, giving them a competitive advantage.

Moreover, governments are investing in the development of infrastructure to support sustainable transportation startups. This includes the construction of charging stations for electric vehicles, the expansion of bike lanes in urban areas, and the integration of smart transportation systems. By investing in infrastructure, governments create an environment that is conducive to the growth and success of startups in the sustainable transportation sector.

In conclusion, government policies and regulations play a crucial role in supporting sustainable transportation startups. Financial incentives, public procurement preferences, regulations, and infrastructure development are all part of the government's toolkit to encourage and foster innovation in the transportation sector. Startups in the future of transportation niche should remain informed about these policies and regulations to take full advantage of the support available to them. With governments actively supporting and promoting sustainable transportation, startups have a unique opportunity to drive disruption and pave the way for a greener, more sustainable future.

Chapter 6: The Future of Air Transportation

Advances in Aviation Technology

In the fast-paced world of transportation, aviation has always been at the forefront of innovation. Over the years, technological advancements in aviation have revolutionized the way we travel, making it faster, safer, and more efficient. This subchapter explores the latest breakthroughs in aviation technology and their implications for startups in the transportation industry.

One of the most significant advancements in aviation technology is the development of electric aircraft. With the growing concern for environmental sustainability, electric aviation presents a game-changing solution. Startups specializing in electric aircraft are paving the way for a greener future, reducing carbon emissions and noise pollution. Companies like Zunum Aero and Lilium have already made significant progress in designing electric planes for short-haul flights, promising to transform regional air travel.

Furthermore, the advent of autonomous aircraft is transforming the landscape of aviation. Startups are actively exploring the possibilities of self-flying planes, which could increase safety, efficiency, and reduce the need for human pilots. With the integration of artificial intelligence and advanced sensors, autonomous aircraft have the potential to minimize human error and improve overall flight performance. Companies like Kitty

Hawk and Airbus are leading the way in this field, focusing on developing autonomous air taxis and drone delivery systems.

Additionally, startups are leveraging advancements in materials science and aerodynamics to create faster and more fuel-efficient aircraft. Lightweight composite materials, such as carbon fiber, are being used to construct aircraft with reduced weight, resulting in improved fuel efficiency and increased range. Furthermore, advancements in aerodynamics are enabling the design of aircraft with reduced drag, allowing for higher speeds and greater fuel economy.

Lastly, startups are also exploring the potential of urban air mobility (UAM) and vertical takeoff and landing (VTOL) aircraft. With increasing urbanization and traffic congestion, UAM presents a viable solution for efficient transportation within cities. VTOL aircraft, such as helicopters and electric air taxis, can take off and land vertically, eliminating the need for runways and expanding the possibilities for urban transportation.

In conclusion, the future of aviation technology holds immense potential for startups in the transportation industry. Electric aircraft, autonomous systems, advanced materials, and UAM are just a few examples of the disruptive innovations reshaping aviation. By embracing these advancements, startups can contribute to a sustainable, efficient, and interconnected future of transportation.

Startups Disrupting the Air Transportation Industry

As the world of transportation continues to evolve, startups are playing a pivotal role in disrupting traditional industries and reshaping the future of transportation. In particular, the air transportation industry is experiencing a wave of innovation driven by these dynamic and agile startups. This subchapter explores some of the key startups that are revolutionizing the way we travel through the skies.

One of the most prominent startups in the air transportation space is XYZ Aviation, a company that is developing electric flying taxis. By leveraging advancements in electric propulsion and autonomous technology, XYZ Aviation aims to provide a sustainable and efficient mode of transportation within cities. These flying taxis have the potential to alleviate traffic congestion and reduce carbon emissions, making urban transportation more accessible and environmentally friendly.

Another notable startup, AeroDrone, is focused on utilizing unmanned aerial vehicles (UAVs) for package delivery. By capitalizing on the growing demand for fast and efficient delivery services, AeroDrone is developing a network of autonomous drones that can transport goods over long distances. This innovative approach to logistics has the potential to revolutionize the e-commerce industry and transform the way we receive our packages.

Additionally, AirBnB for Airplanes, a startup founded on the sharing economy model, is disrupting the private aviation industry. By connecting aircraft owners with travelers in need of private flights, AirBnB for Airplanes is democratizing air travel and making it more accessible to a wider audience. This platform not only benefits travelers by providing more affordable options, but it also allows aircraft owners to monetize their assets when they are not in use.

Lastly, Skyscape Technologies is revolutionizing air traffic management and safety. By leveraging artificial intelligence and data analytics, Skyscape Technologies is creating a smart air traffic control system that can optimize flight routes, prevent collisions, and improve overall safety. This startup has the potential to transform the way air traffic is managed, making air transportation more efficient and reliable.

These startups are just a few examples of the groundbreaking innovation happening within the air transportation industry. By challenging traditional norms and embracing new technologies, these startups are paving the way for a future of transportation that is more sustainable, efficient, and accessible. As a startup in the transportation niche, it is crucial to stay abreast of these disruptive trends and consider how you can contribute to this exciting transformation.

Challenges and Opportunities for Air Transportation Startups

The air transportation industry has long been dominated by established players with deep pockets and extensive resources. However, in recent years, the emergence of startups in this sector has disrupted the status quo and opened up new opportunities for innovation and growth. This subchapter explores the challenges and opportunities faced by air transportation startups, offering valuable insights for entrepreneurs looking to make their mark in the future of transportation.

One of the primary challenges for air transportation startups is the high cost of entry. Building and maintaining an aircraft fleet, acquiring the necessary permits and certifications, and meeting stringent safety regulations require substantial capital investment. Moreover, the industry's complex and bureaucratic nature can pose barriers to entry for newcomers. However, advancements in technology and the rise of shared economy models have created new avenues for startups to overcome these challenges.

One of the most significant opportunities for air transportation startups lies in the growing demand for sustainable and eco-friendly travel options. With increasing concerns about carbon emissions and environmental impact, there is a rising need for innovative solutions that can reduce the industry's ecological footprint. Startups that focus on developing electric or hybrid aircraft, biofuels, or other sustainable aviation technologies can tap into this emerging market and gain a competitive edge.

Another key opportunity lies in leveraging emerging technologies to enhance customer experience and operational efficiency. The integration of artificial intelligence, machine learning, and data analytics can help startups optimize flight routes, improve maintenance processes, and personalize passenger services. By harnessing these technologies, startups can differentiate themselves from traditional airlines and offer unique value propositions.

Additionally, the rise of urban air mobility presents a promising opportunity for startups. The concept of flying taxis or autonomous aerial vehicles for short-distance urban transportation is gaining traction. Startups that can develop and operate these aerial mobility solutions stand to benefit from the increasing demand for efficient, time-saving transportation options in congested cities.

Collaboration and partnerships are also essential for air transportation startups to thrive. By partnering with established industry players, startups can access valuable expertise, resources, and market reach. Building strategic alliances with regulatory bodies, airports, and infrastructure providers can also help overcome regulatory hurdles and infrastructure limitations.

In conclusion, while air transportation startups face significant challenges in terms of high entry costs and regulatory complexities, there are ample opportunities for those willing to disrupt the industry. By focusing on sustainability, leveraging emerging technologies, exploring urban air mobility, and forging strategic partnerships, startups can carve a niche in the future of transportation. This subchapter aims to inspire and guide aspiring entrepreneurs in this space, providing insights into the challenges they may encounter and the opportunities that await them.

Chapter 7: Hyperloop and Other Innovative Transportation Technologies

Understanding Hyperloop Technology

In recent years, an innovative transportation concept has been making waves in the industry and capturing the imagination of startups and transportation enthusiasts alike. Hyperloop technology, first proposed by Elon Musk in 2013, has the potential to revolutionize the future of transportation. This subchapter aims to provide startups in the transportation niche with a comprehensive understanding of this groundbreaking technology.

Hyperloop is a high-speed transportation system that utilizes a network of low-pressure tubes to transport pods or capsules at incredible speeds. By eliminating air resistance and friction, the Hyperloop concept promises to achieve speeds of up to 700 mph, significantly faster than any existing mode of transportation. This not only reduces travel time but also opens up opportunities for faster and more efficient transportation of goods and people.

The core technology behind Hyperloop involves a combination of magnetic levitation (maglev) and reduced pressure tubes. The pods, or capsules, are propelled through the tubes using a combination of electric motors and magnetic forces. This unique combination allows for a smooth and energy-efficient transportation experience.

One of the key advantages of Hyperloop technology is its potential to be environmentally friendly. With pods traveling in a low-pressure environment, the energy required to move them is significantly reduced compared to traditional transportation systems. Additionally, the use of electric motors eliminates direct carbon emissions, making it a promising solution for sustainable transportation.

The potential applications of Hyperloop technology are vast and varied. From long-distance passenger travel to high-speed freight transportation, the possibilities are endless. Startups in the transportation niche can explore various business opportunities within the Hyperloop ecosystem, such as pod manufacturing, infrastructure development, and system integration.

However, it is important to note that Hyperloop technology is still in its early stages of development. Several challenges, such as safety regulations, cost-effectiveness, and scalability, need to be addressed before widespread implementation can occur. Nonetheless, numerous startups and established companies are actively working towards overcoming these hurdles and making Hyperloop a reality.

In conclusion, Hyperloop technology holds immense potential for disrupting the future of transportation. Startups in the transportation niche should closely monitor its development and explore the opportunities it presents. By understanding the core technology and the challenges involved, startups can position themselves to play a vital role in shaping the future of transportation through Hyperloop innovation.

Other Innovative Transportation Technologies

In addition to the groundbreaking innovations discussed in the previous chapters, there are numerous other cutting-edge technologies that are revolutionizing the future of transportation. These emerging technologies hold immense potential and are creating exciting opportunities for startups in the transportation industry.

1. Hyperloop: One of the most ambitious and futuristic transportation concepts, the hyperloop aims to revolutionize long-distance travel. Proposed by Elon Musk, this high-speed transportation system involves passenger pods traveling through low-pressure tubes at incredible speeds. Startups are actively exploring the development of hyperloop technology, which could potentially enable travel at speeds exceeding 700 miles per hour.

2. Autonomous Delivery Vehicles: As e-commerce continues to rise, the need for efficient and reliable delivery systems is becoming increasingly important. Startups are developing autonomous delivery vehicles, including drones and robots, that can navigate through urban environments to deliver packages. These technologies have the potential to revolutionize last-mile delivery, reducing costs and increasing efficiency.

3. Vertical Takeoff and Landing (VTOL) Aircraft: VTOL aircraft, also known as flying cars or air taxis, are being developed by startups to alleviate traffic congestion and provide rapid transportation in urban areas. These electric-powered aircraft are capable of taking off and landing vertically, allowing them to

operate in tight spaces. Companies are exploring various models, including piloted and autonomous VTOLs, with the aim of creating a new mode of transportation.

4. Electric Vertical Takeoff and Landing (eVTOL) Aircraft: Similar to VTOLs, eVTOLs are electric-powered aircraft designed for short takeoff and landing. These aircraft are quieter, more energy-efficient, and produce zero emissions, making them a promising option for urban transportation. Startups are working on eVTOL prototypes that can transport passengers and goods, offering a sustainable alternative to traditional aircraft.

5. Maglev Trains: Magnetic levitation (maglev) trains use magnetic forces to propel and suspend the train above the tracks, eliminating friction and allowing for incredibly high speeds. Startups are exploring the development of maglev trains that can reach speeds of over 300 miles per hour, revolutionizing long-distance travel and reducing travel times significantly.

These are just a few examples of the many innovative transportation technologies that are reshaping the future of mobility. Startups in the transportation industry have a unique opportunity to drive disruption and be at the forefront of these technological advancements. By harnessing these emerging technologies, startups can create sustainable and efficient transportation solutions that meet the evolving needs of society. The future of transportation is being shaped by the creativity and ingenuity of startups, and the possibilities are endless.

Startups Pioneering Hyperloop and Innovative Transportation Solutions

In recent years, the transportation industry has been undergoing a significant transformation, driven by technological advancements and a growing need for sustainable and efficient solutions. Startups have emerged as the key players in this disruption, pushing the boundaries of what was once thought impossible. One such revolutionary concept that has gained immense traction is the Hyperloop.

The Hyperloop, initially proposed by Elon Musk in 2013, envisions a futuristic mode of transportation that could propel passengers at high speeds through near-vacuum tubes. This concept has captured the imagination of numerous startups worldwide, who are now working tirelessly to make it a reality. These startups are not only focusing on the technical and engineering challenges of building the Hyperloop, but also exploring the potential of this transportation system to revolutionize intercity and even international travel.

By developing innovative technologies, startups are paving the way for a future where transportation is faster, more efficient, and environmentally friendly. They are leveraging advancements in materials science, propulsion systems, and autonomous technology to create disruptive solutions that could reshape the way we move people and goods.

In addition to the Hyperloop, startups are also exploring other ground-breaking transportation solutions. Electric and autonomous vehicles have become hotbeds for innovation, with numerous startups developing cutting-edge technologies to make these concepts a reality. From self-driving taxis to electric-powered long-haul trucks, these startups are reimagining transportation from the ground up.

Furthermore, startups are also revolutionizing the last-mile delivery industry. With the rise of e-commerce, the demand for efficient and sustainable solutions to deliver packages has never been higher. Startups are experimenting with drones, robots, and other autonomous delivery systems to meet this demand, promising faster and more cost-effective delivery options.

The future of transportation lies in the hands of startups who dare to challenge the status quo and think beyond traditional means. Their disruptive ideas and relentless pursuit of innovative solutions are reshaping the industry and creating opportunities for a more sustainable, efficient, and interconnected world. As a startup in the transportation space, it is crucial to stay abreast of these pioneering initiatives and collaborate with like-minded innovators to drive the industry forward.

In this subchapter, we will explore the startups at the forefront of Hyperloop development, as well as those developing groundbreaking technologies in electric and autonomous vehicles and last-mile delivery solutions. By understanding their approaches, successes, and challenges, you will gain valuable insights into the future of transportation and how your startup can play a role in shaping it.

Chapter 8: Funding and Investment Opportunities for Transportation Startups

Sources of Funding for Transportation Startups

As the transportation industry continues to undergo significant disruption and innovation, startups are playing a crucial role in shaping the future of transportation. However, one of the biggest challenges that transportation startups face is securing adequate funding to fuel their growth and development. In this subchapter, we will explore the various sources of funding available to transportation startups, enabling them to turn their ideas into reality.

1. Venture Capital (VC) Funding: VC firms are actively seeking out startups in the transportation sector, recognizing the immense potential for growth and disruption. These firms invest in early-stage startups with high growth potential in exchange for equity stakes. Transportation startups can leverage VC funding to support their product development, marketing efforts, and market expansion.

2. Angel Investors: Angel investors are individuals who provide capital to startups in exchange for equity ownership. These individuals often have expertise in the transportation industry and can bring valuable industry insights and connections to the table. Transportation startups can approach angel investors who share their vision and have a track record of supporting disruptive ventures.

3. Crowdfunding: Crowdfunding platforms have gained popularity as a means of raising funds for startups. Transportation startups can use platforms like Kickstarter or Indiegogo to pitch their ideas to a wide audience, allowing interested individuals to contribute funds in exchange for early access to products or other perks. Crowdfunding not only provides funding but also serves as a marketing tool, helping startups build a community and generate awareness about their innovations.

4. Government Grants and Programs: Many governments and public agencies offer grants and funding programs specifically targeted at transportation startups. These grants aim to support the development of sustainable, efficient, and innovative transportation solutions. Startups can explore government initiatives at local, regional, and national levels to secure funding for research, development, and pilot projects.

5. Incubators and Accelerators: Joining an incubator or accelerator program can provide transportation startups with access to funding, mentorship, and networking opportunities. These programs offer a supportive environment for startups to grow and refine their ideas, often culminating in demo days where startups can pitch to potential investors and secure additional funding.

6. Corporate Partnerships: Transportation startups can seek partnerships and collaborations with established companies in the industry. These partnerships can provide startups with access to

funding, resources, expertise, and distribution channels. Working with corporate partners can also lend credibility to transportation startups and open doors to additional funding opportunities.

In conclusion, funding is a critical component for transportation startups to thrive and drive disruption in the industry. By exploring options such as venture capital, angel investors, crowdfunding, government grants, incubators, accelerators, and corporate partnerships, transportation startups can secure the necessary resources to bring their innovative ideas to life and shape the future of transportation.

Key Considerations for Investors in the Transportation Industry

As startups continue to pave the way for the future of transportation, it is crucial for investors to carefully evaluate their investment opportunities in this rapidly evolving industry. The transportation industry is undergoing a significant transformation, driven by technological advancements, changing consumer preferences, and the need for sustainable and efficient solutions. In this subchapter, we will discuss the key considerations that investors should keep in mind when investing in startups within the transportation industry.

1. Technological Disruption: The transportation industry is experiencing a wave of technological disruption, with innovations such as autonomous vehicles, electric mobility, and the sharing economy reshaping the landscape. Investors should closely examine startups that leverage these disruptive technologies and have a clear value proposition and competitive advantage.

2. Market Potential: Assessing the market potential is crucial for investors. They should evaluate startups operating within niche markets of the future of transportation, such as electric scooters, urban air mobility, or last-mile delivery. Understanding the market size, growth potential, and competitive landscape will help investors make informed investment decisions.

3. Regulatory Environment: The transportation industry is heavily regulated, and investors need to understand the regulatory challenges that startups may face. Evaluating startups' strategies for navigating complex regulations, obtaining necessary permits,

and ensuring compliance is essential. Additionally, keeping an eye on any potential regulatory changes or advancements is crucial to stay ahead of the curve.

4. Sustainability and Environmental Impact: With increasing concerns about climate change and environmental sustainability, investors should prioritize startups that offer sustainable transportation solutions. Startups focused on electric vehicles, alternative fuels, or reducing carbon emissions are likely to attract more attention from environmentally conscious investors.

5. Business Model and Scalability: Investors should assess the startups' business models and their potential for scalability. Startups that offer innovative, scalable, and profitable business models are more likely to succeed in the long run. Evaluating their revenue streams, cost structures, and growth strategies will help investors determine their potential for profitability and success.

6. Team and Expertise: Lastly, investors should evaluate the team behind the startup. Assessing the founders' industry knowledge, experience, and track record is crucial. Startups with a strong, diverse team that possesses the necessary skills and expertise are more likely to navigate the challenges of the transportation industry successfully.

In summary, investing in startups within the transportation industry requires careful consideration of various factors. By evaluating technological disruption, market potential, regulatory environment, sustainability, business models, and the team, investors can make informed decisions and contribute to shaping the future of transportation.

Success Stories and Lessons from Successful Transportation Startups

In this subchapter, we delve into the inspiring success stories and invaluable lessons learned from transportation startups that have revolutionized the industry. These startups have not only disrupted traditional modes of transportation but have also paved the way for the future of the industry. As startups in the transportation sector, understanding and learning from their experiences can provide valuable insights and guidance for your own entrepreneurial journey.

One remarkable success story is that of Uber, which single-handedly transformed the taxi industry. By leveraging technology and providing a seamless user experience through a mobile app, Uber disrupted traditional taxi services by offering convenience, affordability, and efficiency. The lesson here is to embrace technology and constantly innovate to meet the evolving needs of customers.

Another notable success story is Tesla, the electric vehicle (EV) manufacturer. Tesla's visionary founder, Elon Musk, demonstrated that EVs can be both practical and luxurious, challenging the perception that electric cars are not viable alternatives to traditional combustion engine vehicles. Tesla's success highlights the importance of challenging the status quo, pushing boundaries, and investing in sustainable and eco-friendly solutions.

Furthermore, the rise of micro-mobility startups like Bird and Lime has showcased the potential of electric scooters and bicycles in urban transportation. These startups have successfully provided last-mile solutions, addressing the challenges of congestion and pollution in cities. The key takeaway from these success stories is the importance of identifying niche opportunities and offering innovative solutions that cater to specific transportation needs.

In addition to success stories, it is equally important to learn from failures. Startups like Sidecar and Chariot, which attempted to disrupt the ride-sharing and shuttle services respectively, could not sustain their operations in the long run. These failures emphasize the need for startups to have a sustainable business model, adapt to changing market dynamics, and continuously iterate based on user feedback.

To succeed in the future of transportation, startups need to embrace emerging technologies such as artificial intelligence, autonomous vehicles, and the Internet of Things. By leveraging these technologies, startups can create safer, more efficient, and sustainable transportation solutions.

In conclusion, the success stories and lessons from these transportation startups offer invaluable insights and inspiration for entrepreneurs in the ever-evolving industry. By understanding the strategies, challenges, and innovations that have fueled their success, startups can navigate the complex landscape of the future of transportation. Embrace technology, challenge the status quo, identify niche opportunities, learn from failures, and leverage emerging technologies to drive disruption and pave the way for the future of transportation.

Chapter 9: Overcoming Challenges and Building a Successful Transportation Startup

Identifying and Addressing Market Needs

In the fast-paced world of transportation, startups play a crucial role in driving innovation and shaping the future. As a startup in the transportation industry, understanding and addressing market needs is essential for success. This subchapter delves into the importance of identifying these needs and provides insights on how to effectively address them.

To thrive in the ever-evolving landscape of transportation, startups must have a clear understanding of the market they aim to serve. Identifying market needs involves conducting thorough research and analysis to gain insights into customer demands, pain points, and emerging trends. By staying ahead of the curve, startups can position themselves as pioneers in the industry and develop solutions that truly meet the market's requirements.

One strategy to identify market needs is to engage in customer discovery. This involves actively listening to potential customers, conducting surveys, and gathering feedback to gain a deep understanding of their expectations. By empathizing with their challenges, startups can tailor their products or services to meet these needs effectively.

Additionally, monitoring industry trends and advancements is crucial for identifying emerging market needs. Through constant market analysis, startups can identify gaps and opportunities that can be transformed into disruptive innovations. Staying informed about technological advancements, regulatory changes, and shifting consumer preferences will enable startups to anticipate market needs and adjust their strategies accordingly.

Once market needs are identified, addressing them becomes the next crucial step. Startups must focus on developing innovative solutions that fill these gaps and create value for their target audience. This may involve utilizing cutting-edge technologies such as artificial intelligence, blockchain, or electric mobility to revolutionize the transportation industry.

Furthermore, startups should prioritize customer-centricity when addressing market needs. By continuously engaging with customers, understanding their pain points, and incorporating their feedback into product development, startups can build long-lasting relationships and foster loyalty. This customer-focused approach will not only help address immediate market needs but also allow for continuous improvement and adaptation as the industry evolves.

In conclusion, identifying and addressing market needs is paramount for startups in the future of transportation niche. By conducting comprehensive market research, engaging in customer discovery, and staying abreast of industry trends, startups can gain a competitive edge and create disruptive solutions. By prioritizing customer-centricity and continuously adapting to evolving market needs, startups can pave the way for a future where transportation is faster, safer, and more efficient.

Navigating Regulatory Hurdles and Legal Considerations

In the rapidly evolving landscape of transportation, startups face numerous regulatory hurdles and legal considerations. As emerging technologies disrupt traditional modes of transportation, it is crucial for startups to understand the legal framework and regulatory landscape to ensure compliance, mitigate risks, and unlock the full potential of their innovations.

1. Understanding the Regulatory Landscape: Startups in the future of transportation niche must familiarize themselves with the regulatory bodies and laws that govern their industry. This includes understanding transportation regulations at both the local and national levels. From autonomous vehicles to drone delivery systems, startups need to understand the legal requirements and obtain necessary permits, licenses, and certifications to operate legally.

2. Navigating Safety and Liability Concerns: Safety is a paramount concern in the transportation industry. Startups need to address safety and liability considerations to gain public trust and ensure the smooth operation of their services. This involves conducting thorough risk assessments, implementing safety protocols, and having proper insurance coverage to protect against potential accidents or damages.

3. Privacy and Data Protection: As startups collect and utilize vast amounts of data to optimize their transportation services, they must also prioritize privacy and data protection. Complying with data protection laws, ensuring

secure data storage, and obtaining necessary consents from users are critical steps to avoid legal pitfalls and maintain customer trust.

4.	Intellectual	Property	Protection: Innovations in the future of transportation often involve novel technologies, algorithms, or designs. Startups must secure intellectual property rights through patents, trademarks, or copyrights to protect their innovations from infringement and maintain a competitive edge. Understanding the nuances of intellectual property law and working closely with legal experts is essential in this process.

5.	Collaborating	with	Regulators: Startups should engage in proactive dialogue with regulatory bodies to shape policies and regulations that accommodate innovative transportation solutions. Building strong relationships with regulators can help streamline the approval process, identify potential roadblocks, and foster an environment conducive to growth and innovation.

6.	Staying	Agile	and	Adaptable: Regulatory frameworks can change rapidly, particularly in the dynamic field of transportation. Startups must stay agile and adaptable to navigate evolving regulations. This may involve monitoring legislative developments, seeking legal counsel when needed, and being prepared to adjust business strategies to comply with new requirements.

Navigating regulatory hurdles and legal considerations is an ongoing challenge for startups in the future of transportation niche. By understanding the regulatory landscape, prioritizing safety and privacy, protecting intellectual property, collaborating with regulators, and remaining agile, startups can position themselves for success while driving disruptive change in the transportation industry.

Strategies for Growth and Scaling in the Transportation Industry

Introduction:

As startups in the transportation industry, it is crucial to understand the strategies that can help you achieve growth and scale your business effectively. In this subchapter, we will discuss some key strategies that can pave the way for your success in the future of transportation.

1. Embrace Technological Advancements: The future of transportation is heavily reliant on technology, so it is vital for startups to embrace innovative technologies. Invest in research and development to stay ahead of the curve and integrate emerging technologies such as artificial intelligence, machine learning, and Internet of Things in your transportation solutions. By leveraging these advancements, you can offer more efficient, cost-effective, and sustainable transportation options, setting yourself apart from competitors.

2. Collaborate with Established Players: Collaborating with established players in the transportation industry can provide startups with valuable resources, expertise, and market access. Partnering with established companies, such as automakers or logistics providers, can help you tap into their existing customer base and gain credibility. Additionally, collaboration can also lead to knowledge sharing and joint ventures, enabling startups to scale their operations faster.

3.   Focus   on   Customer   Experience:
In the future of transportation, customer experience will be a key differentiator. Startups should prioritize understanding their target audience's needs and expectations and design their services to cater to them. By providing personalized, convenient, and seamless transportation experiences, you can build a loyal customer base and generate positive word-of-mouth, leading to organic growth.

4.   Expand   to   New   Markets:
To achieve growth and scale, startups must explore new markets and expand their geographical reach. Conduct thorough market research to identify untapped opportunities, both domestically and internationally. Consider partnering with local players or adapting your business model to suit specific markets' needs. Expanding to new markets can not only increase revenue but also diversify risk and reduce dependence on a single market.

5.   Build   a   Strong   Team:
A successful startup in the transportation industry needs a talented and dedicated team. Hire individuals with diverse skill sets, including technology, operations, marketing, and finance. Foster a culture of innovation, collaboration, and continuous learning within your organization. A strong team can help you execute your growth strategies effectively and overcome challenges along the way.

Conclusion:

As startups in the future of transportation, implementing these strategies can lay the foundation for your growth and scaling. Embrace technology, collaborate with established players, prioritize customer experience, expand to new markets, and build a strong team. By following these strategies, you can position your startup for success in the dynamic and evolving transportation industry.

Chapter 10: The Future of Transportation: Predictions and Possibilities

Emerging Trends and Technologies in Transportation

In today's fast-paced world, transportation has become a critical aspect of our daily lives. From commuting to work to exploring new destinations, the way we move has a profound impact on our personal and professional lives. As startups and entrepreneurs, it is crucial to stay ahead of the curve and embrace the emerging trends and technologies that are shaping the future of transportation.

One of the most significant trends revolutionizing transportation is the rise of electric vehicles (EVs). With increasing concerns about climate change and the need to reduce greenhouse gas emissions, EVs have gained immense popularity. Startups focused on developing EV technologies and infrastructure have the potential to disrupt the traditional automobile industry. From innovative battery technologies to charging stations, there is a vast scope for startups to contribute to the future of transportation through electric mobility.

Another emerging trend in transportation is the concept of shared mobility. With the advent of ride-sharing platforms like Uber and Lyft, the way we travel has transformed. Startups that focus on shared mobility solutions such as carpooling, bike-sharing, and scooter-sharing have the potential to reduce traffic congestion, lower transportation costs, and improve overall efficiency. By utilizing technology and data analytics, startups can create platforms that connect riders and drivers, optimizing the use of vehicles and reducing the number of cars on the road.

The integration of artificial intelligence (AI) and machine learning (ML) algorithms in transportation is yet another trend worth mentioning. Startups can leverage AI and ML to develop smart transportation systems that enhance safety, efficiency, and connectivity. For instance, autonomous vehicles are becoming a reality, with companies like Tesla and Waymo leading the way. Startups can contribute by developing AI-powered navigation systems, advanced driver assistance systems (ADAS), and predictive maintenance solutions, among others.

Furthermore, the use of drones in transportation is an emerging technology that holds immense potential. Startups can explore the use of drones for last-mile delivery, infrastructure inspections, and emergency response, among other applications. By leveraging drones, startups can overcome logistical challenges, reduce delivery times, and improve overall efficiency in the transportation sector.

In conclusion, the future of transportation is being shaped by exciting trends and technologies that offer immense opportunities for startups. Whether it is electric vehicles, shared mobility, AI and ML integration, or the use of drones, entrepreneurs in the transportation niche have a chance to disrupt traditional models and pave the way for a more sustainable, efficient, and connected future. By embracing these emerging trends and technologies, startups can drive the disruption needed to transform the transportation industry as we know it.

Potential Impacts on Society and the Economy

As startups continue to innovate and disrupt traditional modes of transportation, the potential impacts on society and the economy are substantial. The future of transportation holds exciting possibilities for startups, and understanding the potential implications is crucial for those operating in this space.

One of the most significant impacts on society is the potential for increased accessibility and convenience. Startups are developing technologies that aim to bridge the gap between different modes of transportation, making it easier for individuals to navigate their daily lives. For example, ride-sharing platforms have already transformed the way people commute, reducing the need for personal vehicle ownership and decreasing traffic congestion. As these services continue to evolve and integrate with other modes of transportation, the overall accessibility and convenience for individuals will improve significantly.

Furthermore, startups in the transportation sector have the potential to revolutionize urban planning and infrastructure. Electric and autonomous vehicles, for instance, have the capacity to reshape cities. With reduced reliance on fossil fuels and increased efficiency, these vehicles can contribute to a cleaner environment and reduce carbon emissions. Additionally, the advent of autonomous vehicles has the potential to transform parking spaces, as self-driving cars can drop off passengers and find parking spaces outside of city centers. This development could free up valuable urban real estate for other purposes, such as parks or affordable housing.

From an economic standpoint, startups in the future of transportation niche can create significant job opportunities. As new technologies emerge, there will be a need for skilled professionals to design, develop, and maintain these innovations. Startups that pioneer these advancements will not only benefit from the economic growth generated by their own operations but also contribute to job creation in related industries.

At the same time, the disruption caused by startups may pose challenges to certain sectors of the economy. For instance, traditional taxi services and car manufacturers may face declining demand as ride-sharing and electric vehicles become more prevalent. However, there will also be opportunities for these established players to adapt and collaborate with startups, ensuring their continued relevance in the evolving transportation landscape.

In conclusion, startups in the future of transportation have the potential to create significant impacts on society and the economy. Increased accessibility and convenience, environmental benefits, job creation, and urban planning improvements are just a few examples of the transformative potential of these innovations. While challenges and disruptions are to be expected, the overall societal and economic benefits outweigh the drawbacks. By embracing and collaborating with startups, industries and individuals can collectively shape a future of transportation that is more sustainable, efficient, and inclusive.

The Role of Startups in Shaping the Future of Transportation

In an era of fast-paced technological advancements, startups have emerged as the driving force behind transforming the future of transportation. These innovative companies are revolutionizing the way we move, creating sustainable and efficient solutions to address the challenges faced by traditional transportation systems. This subchapter explores the pivotal role startups play in shaping the future of transportation and the incredible opportunities they bring to the table.

Startups have the unique advantage of being nimble and agile, enabling them to adapt quickly to changing market demands and emerging technologies. They have disrupted the transportation industry by introducing innovative concepts such as ride-hailing services, electric vehicles, autonomous vehicles, and shared mobility. These disruptive startups have not only challenged the status quo but have also paved the way for a more sustainable and connected transportation ecosystem.

One of the key contributions of startups in the future of transportation is their emphasis on sustainability. With increasing concerns about climate change and pollution, startups are developing eco-friendly alternatives to traditional modes of transportation. Electric vehicle startups, for instance, are leading the charge in reducing carbon emissions and dependence on fossil fuels. Moreover, startups are also focusing on creating efficient transportation systems that promote shared mobility, reducing congestion and the overall carbon footprint.

Startups are also at the forefront of the autonomous vehicle revolution, developing cutting-edge technologies that have the potential to reshape the way we travel. With the advent of artificial intelligence and machine learning, these startups are working towards creating safe and reliable self-driving vehicles that can significantly improve road safety and efficiency. By leveraging advanced sensors and algorithms, they are paving the way for a future where commuting becomes more productive, enjoyable, and ultimately, accident-free.

Another area where startups are making a significant impact is in urban mobility. As cities face increasing challenges in managing traffic congestion and limited infrastructure, startups are introducing innovative solutions such as bike-sharing, scooter-sharing, and micro-mobility services. These startups are reimagining the last-mile connectivity problem and providing convenient and sustainable alternatives to traditional modes of transportation.

In conclusion, startups are playing a crucial role in shaping the future of transportation. Their disruptive ideas and innovative technologies are revolutionizing the way we move, making transportation more sustainable, efficient, and connected. As startups continue to drive disruption in the transportation industry, they open up new opportunities for collaboration, investment, and growth. It is imperative for startups to seize these opportunities and contribute actively to the future of transportation, as they hold the key to a more sustainable, efficient, and inclusive transportation ecosystem.

Conclusion: Driving Disruption: Startups Leading the Way

Conclusion: Driving Disruption: Startups Leading the Way

The future of transportation is undergoing a massive transformation, and startups are at the forefront of this disruptive change. In this book, we have explored how these innovative companies are paving the way for a new era of transportation, one that is more sustainable, efficient, and connected than ever before. As we conclude our journey through the world of startups and the future of transportation, we are left with a sense of excitement and hope for what lies ahead.

Throughout this book, we have witnessed the incredible strides startups have made in revolutionizing various aspects of transportation. From electric vehicles and autonomous driving to ride-sharing platforms and urban mobility solutions, these startups have challenged the status quo and opened up new possibilities for how we move from one place to another. They have shown us that the future of transportation is not just about getting from point A to point B, but also about creating a seamless and enjoyable experience for passengers.

Startups have proven to be the driving force behind many disruptive technologies and business models in the transportation industry. Their nimbleness, agility, and willingness to take risks have allowed them to quickly adapt and innovate in an industry that has historically been slow to change. By challenging traditional players and introducing new ideas, startups have forced the industry to rethink its approach and embrace a more customer-centric mindset.

The future of transportation is not without its challenges, but startups have shown us that they are up to the task. They have demonstrated that it is possible to develop sustainable and environmentally friendly alternatives to fossil fuel-powered vehicles. They have also shown us that autonomous driving can be safe and reliable, paving the way for a future where accidents are a thing of the past. Moreover, startups have proven that by leveraging technology and data, we can optimize transportation systems and reduce congestion in our cities.

As we look ahead, it is clear that startups will continue to play a crucial role in shaping the future of transportation. Their disruptive ideas and innovative solutions will drive us towards a more sustainable and efficient transportation system. However, for startups to succeed, collaboration and partnerships with established players will be essential. By working together, startups and traditional companies can combine their strengths and create a transportation ecosystem that benefits everyone.

In conclusion, startups are leading the way in driving disruption in the transportation industry. They have shown us what is possible and have paved the way for a future that is more connected, sustainable, and efficient. The journey is far from over, but with startups at the helm, we can be confident that the future of transportation is in good hands. Let us embrace this disruptive change and work towards a transportation system that is not only efficient but also enhances the lives of people around the world.